Many Blessings!
Rosemary

Baby Dedication

It's Not About The Baby

ROSEMARY WINBUSH

Baby Dedication

It's Not About The Baby

Baby Dedication   It's Not About The Baby

Copyright © November 12, 2018,
by Rosemary Winbush. All rights reserved.
Kairos International, Jacksonville, Florida

Scripture quotations are taken from the Holy Bible
(various versions).

Printed in the United States of America
ISBN-13:978-1729740644
ISBN-10:1729740642

Deuteronomy 6:5-9

Love the LORD, your God, with all your heart and with all your soul and with all your strength. These commandments that I give you today are to be on your hearts. Impress them on your children. Talk about them when you sit at home and when you walk along the road, when you lie down and when you get up. Tie them as symbols on your hands and bind them on your foreheads. Write them on the doorframes of your houses and on your gates.

This book is a help tool written in hope to give parents and guardians a deeper understanding of Baby Dedication and the ending benefits it can produce in their lives, the lives of their children, their communities, and the life of the Church. It is written from a Biblical perspective with God, Jesus, and Holy Spirit as the central focus in the home.

Thank you

to all the families who have made the decision to dedicate their lives to training up their children to know The Lord and to think like Him.

Baby Dedication 101

Understanding the assignment of the family to reproduce, nurture, and empower the next and now generations of Kingdom citizens.

Congratulations are in order on the birth of a life destined to honor God. There is an excitement like no other when families make a commitment to raise their children to live a life pleasing to The Lord. Devoting one's self to the task and purpose of raising godly children is to be commended. You are celebrated, because you are saying, 'Yes Lord, I will raise my child to know You and Your ways.' You are celebrated, because you have made the decision to be a godly parent and guardian for your child.

You may think the subtitle of this book is strange, but the actual dedication is not about the baby (child). It is about the commitment you as parents and guardians make to The Lord to be good stewards over *His* children. This stewardship goes beyond providing food, clothes, shelter, protection, etc. You are making a covenant with The Lord to honor Him by submitting your will to His Will when it comes to raising children. The results of this dedication journey, however, will benefit the baby (child), but the process of the dedication will be up to you as parents and guardians to complete. If we do what The Lord expects in our dedication process, our children will receive Jesus according to their own faith and will be baptized according to their own desire (Romans 10, Mark 16). Salvation is personal and The Lord wants each of us to make the individual decision to follow Him. This decision to follow Jesus is up to our children, but we play a role in guiding them in biblical truths, demonstrating the love of Jesus, and equipping them with the necessary tools to make the one decision which will change their lives eternally.

Baby dedication is NOT a baptism, christening, nor a call to salvation for your child, but it is a commitment you as parents and guardians have made to raise your child with the benefit of knowing The Lord, our God. You have made a commitment to tell your child about God, the Father; God, the Son; and God, the Holy Spirit. You have made a commitment to live a life holy before your child which demonstrates the life of a true Believer. You have made a decision to become the primary leader in the discipleship process of your child.

The ceremony of a baby dedication is the church witnessing your promise to God to reproduce another Believer in the earth who will honor and live for Him. You will point your child to Jesus Christ, the Son of God and Savior of the world by yielding to the direction and guidance of Holy Spirit. You are promising to add value to the Kingdom by training your child to become a Kingdom citizen knowing the full truth of the Gospel which will help them in their commitment to carry out the discipleship plan and commission of Jesus Christ (Matthew 28).

A baby dedication ceremony may consist of anointing the entire family with oil, which represents blessings as families carry out this assignment. The oil anointing also symbolizes our faith in the power and guidance of Holy Spirit, who is available to help us along the journey. The goal of the ceremony is to bless and cover you and your child through prayer and support as you walk in the charge to lead in the spiritual maturity of your child.

Those of us who serve in ministry to children consider it an honor to partner with families as they raise their children in the admonition of The Lord. We thank you for allowing us the opportunity to join forces with you to teach your child about the love and saving grace of Jesus Christ. But understand, the church is a support to families and does not take on the full responsibility concerning the spiritual growth of the child. This responsibility is given to families with the support of the church. It is important to find a local church fellowship able to support you as you raise your child in the faith. Search and vet church fellowships to find the best fit for your entire family.

Raising children is not an easy task, but with the help of The Lord and surrounding yourself with others in the faith, you are well able to do it. Whatever happens in the journey of parenthood, remember, you are not alone. Asking for help and knowing where to get help is half the battle. We can always go to God and ask for help and there will be others God has assigned to help in raising your child. When things happen, whether good or bad, remember you are probably not the first it has happened to and you are probably not going to be the last it will happen to. The important thing to know is you have access to the wisdom and knowledge of an eternal God who knows everything about you and your child. The Bible is your help instruction book and the guide to understanding God's plan for your lives. Knowing what it says and teaching your child what it says will give you both access to the keys of the Kingdom.

It has been proven that parents and family members are the most influential people in a child's life, especially during their developmental years. Parents and guardians must model behaviors which exemplify a faithful and committed Believer in Jesus Christ. As Believers, we are charged in Matthew 28 to make disciples. This is a charge for every parent and guardian to disciple their household. So, guard your influence making sure it reflects the things of God. There are stories in the Bible when entire households were saved because of the influence of one family member. Noah's household was saved, because he was faithfulness to The Lord (Genesis 7:1). The household of the nation of Nineveh was saved, because the King and the people repented after Jonah's warning (Jonah 3:6-10). The household of the Philippian jailer was saved, because he believed in the God of Paul and Silas (Acts 16:25-34). Peter is sent to Cornelius's house to testify about the works of Jesus, and Cornelius's entire household was saved because he believed (Acts 10). Because of your willingness to obey God in the commitment of this dedication, He will make provision for the salvation of your household.

If we are unintentional when it comes to the preparation of sharing the Gospel with our children, we risk the loss of our own households and this would truly be a great tragedy. We must be intentional and become prepared for this assignment. The Lord wants every home to honor Him. The Lord wants our homes to be the training camps for Kingdom warriors and citizens.

Creating an environment in our homes that breed love, respect, and honor towards God is vital in the dedication process. Our children will typically embrace what we embrace. So, make sure the atmosphere around you reflects the attitude and culture embraced by God. When we create this environment, the entire family will know Jesus is the center of what we believe and every family member will have a general understanding of the family vision and belief system (Proverbs 22).

Proverbs 22:6, *"Train up a child in the way he should go, And even when he is old he will not depart from it.*

Ephesians 6:4 challenges parents not to provoke their children to wrath, but to bring them up in the nurture and admonition of The Lord. As you work towards your own Christian discipleship growth, you will experience a greater presence of The Lord in your life and in your home. As you walk closer with The Lord, you will hear His voice clearer, and develop a divine intimacy with Him. As you seek The Lord, He will allow you to find Him. In finding out more about The Lord, you will begin to see things more like He sees them. As you see through the lenses of God, He will begin to show you His ways when it comes to raising your child. This kind of growth will empower your child's growth to see things God's way. When this happens, we can see the fruits of our labor through our own salvation. As your family continues to grow in the grace and knowledge of our Savior and Lord, Jesus Christ, you will be able to discern when things get off track with your family. You will then have the wisdom to seek God and recognize ways to be drawn back into an intimate place of alignment with the Father.

When you dive into the baby dedication process, know that you *will* be tested and you *will* be challenged, but you are designed to do this. You are a protector, developer, and Kingdom builder. You have access to every tool needed to equip your child for Kingdom purpose. Don't give excuses, don't get weary in well doing, and don't listen to the voice of the enemy concerning your child or your abilities. God is with you and you can do this!

The fundamentals of dedicating your life to raise your child in the ways of The Lord will reveal some do's and don'ts. Do not live a life of compromise. Do not live in false realms that distort the Word of God. Do not live to please your flesh. Do not lean unto your own understanding, but look to God for answers. Be true to God and obey His commands for He alone can offer us the true plan of life, because He is the creator of all life. When we live outside the Will of God, we step away from the *full* blessings and covering of The Lord. Getting in position and in the right posture to honor God puts us in alignment with opportunities to be used and blessed by the Him.

There are three (3) general concepts to help guide families in their dedication process. As you approach these three concepts, remember whatever the makeup of your family (married, single, extended family, adoption, blended), you are still a family and have a responsibility to reproduce souls who will know The Lord and live for Him.

Concept 1

What is the purpose of Baby Dedication?

One of the main purposes of baby dedication is to keep your family and it's legacy off the casualty list. As we focus on the biblical meaning of parenting, it is to get the family in position to reproduce others who will honor and serve The Lord. Parenting reflects the leadership in the home. The ability to parent under the deputized authority and love of Jesus Christ gives parents and guardians the right to act as Kingdom ambassadors to reproduce and train others in God's way. This serves as a three-fold purpose: 1) raising a generation who will know and honor God, 2) raising a generation who will receive salvation, and 3) raising a generation who will carry the mantle to repopulate God's family concept throughout time. If we take this mandate casually and not truly focus on the call of being godly parents, we will have casualties in a war we are unaware of.

The following passage is from the book **Essentials to Start, Build and Refresh Children's Ministry by Rosemary Winbush.** As you read this passage, let it transform your thinking about your parenting purpose and how your parenting protects and grooms your child for Kingdom success.

Children represent the young population of the world today and the population of adults of the world for the tomorrows. Every day and every moment a child turns into an adult. Children are the world's most precious commodity. They are a gift from God (Psalm 127:3). Unfortunately, they are not always recognized as such. Children have been abused, mistreated, devalued, murdered, and set aside as lower class citizens. As we raise children, I am reminded of a story of a young prince being trained to rule over a kingdom he would soon possess. As most young princes would have attendants, so did this young prince. Those assigned to the young prince were very attentive. They taught him everything a great and powerful king had to know. They exposed him to the tricks of potential enemies, the tactics of war, and the benefits of living in peace with other kingdoms. They trained him to be disciplined and to think of others (his subjects) over himself. They trained him to be an intellectual and to seek wisdom. The young prince was taught of the riches of his ancestral past and how to grow and manage the wealth of the future kingdom. Throughout his life and training, he was well cared for and protected because of his future purpose. Careful thought and consideration was put in every measure to make sure the young prince would be well equipped to become an effective king and leader. We must look at each child as the young prince. Preparing children to rule with authority given through Jesus Christ is part of their training. We must equip children by revealing to them they are loved by the Lord, they have salvation available to them through Jesus Christ, and they are the sons, daughters, and children of God. When they understand who God is, who Jesus is, and who the Holy Spirit is, they will understand who they are and know the will of the Father for their lives. As Believers, we have a Father in Heaven, who wants sons and daughters who are well able to rule in His Kingdom.

CHILDREN

Cultivating a child's heart for an intimate relationship with the Lord through prayer, the power of the Holy Spirit, and what we speak over their lives can transform the face of the planet. We have an important assignment. Jesus even said, "do not hinder little children but let them come to Him." (Matthew 19:14, Luke 18:16, Mark 10:14) In order to do this, we must be determined to pour the Word of God into the hearts and minds of children with consistency and persistency. Stay focused on the purpose of ministering to children and leading them to Jesus Christ. The Lord has positioned us to nurture the souls of His little ones.

When we minister to children, we must minister knowing their survival depends on it. Their eternal souls are at stake. In Revelation 12:4a, 17 is says, "The dragon stood in front of the woman who was about to give birth, so that it might devour her child the moment he was born." "Then the dragon was enraged at the woman and went off to wage war against the rest of her offspring—those who keep God's commands and hold fast their testimony about Jesus." This is a horrific imagery. The moment children are born, the enemy is after them; and when they live for Jesus, the enemy is after them. We must recognize equipping children is very important. Strategies to disciple and teach authority are survival tools to prepare children to be victorious.

It must be clear that the spiritual growth of children is a priority.

Many people have a misunderstanding about the purpose of baby dedication. They see it as a ritual ceremony to dress their babies in adorn white garments and a formality of religious practices. This is far from the truth. Baby dedication is not a baptism, not a christening, and not a call to salvation for your child. It is an act of parents and guardians making a covenant or vow before the church *to The Lord* to bring up their children with the benefit of knowing God, the creator; the saving grace of Jesus Christ; and the power of Holy Spirit.

In 2 Timothy 3:15, Paul reminded Timothy that from a child he had known the Holy Scriptures. We want this to be true of our children. We want to make sure from their youthful years, we have taught them the Holy Scriptures (Bible/the Word of God), and exposed them to the God who created all things. We want to direct them to God's plan for life. We want to direct them to Jesus, so they will know the Will of the Father and receive Jesus as their Savior and Lord. We want to direct them to walk and engage with Holy Spirit and receive the benefit of a more abundant life. We want them to become followers of Jesus Christ and avoid eternal separation from God.

Children are a gift from God and He has allowed us to be a part of His plan in building His Kingdom (reproducing others in the earth). Partnering with God in His creation is truly an honor.

As we acknowledge God as the giver of all life, we will see how precious to Him the life of a child is. We were all once children; hence, all lives are precious to God. God wants all of us connected to Him. Jesus said in Matthew 19:14, 'Suffer little children, and forbid them not, to come unto me: for of such is the Kingdom of heaven.' Jesus wants us to direct children to Him at the earliest age possible. Through our own dedication to God as adults, we have the greatest opportunity to introduce God, Jesus and Holy Spirit to children.

Studies report by the time a child is nine (9) years old, their core belief system has been established. From 0-3 years old, we have the *greatest opportunity* to share the Gospel of Jesus Christ with children; from 4-6 years old, we have a *greater opportunity* to share the Gospel of Jesus Christ with children; from 7-9 years old, we have a *great opportunity* to share the Gospel of Jesus Christ with children; and from 10 years and up, we have an *opportunity* to share the Gospel of Jesus Christ with children. So, it is in our best interest to give careful consideration to take advantage of the *early exposure concept* by starting with the '*greatest opportunity*' time (0-3 years) to share the Gospel of Jesus Christ with children.

We all want a great crop of children, but are we willing to do the hard work for an extraordinary harvest. What someone did or did not put in us as children strongly reflect who might become. I want to encourage you; all of the hard work and effort of spiritual development we pour into our children is invaluable and worth every sacrifice. You will not regret it.

The children we develop today will be the leaders of tomorrow. We must resolve, as parents or guardians, we choose to contribute to the development of tomorrow's church and community leaders. The quality of our contribution and what we are willing to pour into our children as we train them up will determine the quality of our tomorrows.

Remember, the ceremony of baby dedication has no meaning unless parents and guardians are willing to dedicate themselves to the will of God, our Father.

New Outlook

Write one or two things you have learned about your thinking when it comes to Baby Dedication and how you can change your approach towards dedicating your life to the purpose of Baby Dedication.

_____

_____

_____

_____

_____

_____

_____

Baby Dedication — It's Not About The Baby

Concept 2

How can you prepare for this dedication journey?

Living

Children do what we do, not always what we say. To prepare for this journey, you must be a doer! Allow your children to see you put faith in action. If we want to be people of faith, we must live like people of faith. Engaging with other faith Believers and assembling with other Believers is vital to the preparedness of discipling your child (Hebrews 10:25). Your own spiritual grow can be the shadow of how you child can grow. Let your living be an example by preaching what you practice as well as practicing what you preach.

If you are not engaged and participating in the membership of a local church, now is the time to do so. Find a fellowship where your entire family can grow. If the church has a marriage ministry and you are married, attend sessions and ask questions. A strong marriage based on God's principles provides the best start in creating a nurturing spiritual environment for children. Studies show children who grow up in a mother and father household of Believers, may have less challenges because they have two people reinforcing a biblical lifestyle. If you are a single parent, search out single parenting ministry tips to help you encourage your child to live for Jesus. Remember, even if you are a single parent, you are not alone in raising your child, The Lord is with you and others care about you and your child.

Attending worship services, bible study, marriage/single ministry, and allowing your children/youth to attend special ministry provided for them promotes a *'win win'* situation in family spiritual growth.

Serving
Once you are settled in a local place of worship, find out what ministry opportunities are offered. Pray about how you can contribute to the ministry in serving. Ask God what you are supposed to do in serving. Plan to serve in some capacity. Get involved in ministry, because it will grow you as a Believer.

There are some powerful benefits that come from serving in the view of your children. My husband and I have always served in ministry. Before we were married, we served in ministry. When we had our children, we served in ministry. At the time, we were just doing what God told us. We did not know the impact it would have on our children as they watched us serve. We always invited them to help when they could, and we often explained to them what we were doing and why we were doing it. We rarely missed worship, because we wanted them to know we put a high priority on honoring God in worship, learning, growing and serving. I am thankful to say, they caught the spirit of helping and serving. You see, what they saw us doing, they received it in their hearts and it became a part of them. Now they all serve the Lord for themselves. We were an example, in the working out of our own salvation through serving and being engaged in ministry. We grew and our children grew because of our involvement.

As we served, we were careful to ensure balance. We made sure family was important. Children must know they are loved and appreciated. No one we minster to or help can take the place of the love my husband and I have for our children. I truly believe they know they are loved by The Lord and by us. The affection we have for our children is demonstrated in our actions, prayers, love, and care towards them. Even as young adults, they still know this, because we were intentional. I often remember *thanking* our children, when they were little and as they grew older, for allowing us to serve others without them being jealous of sharing us. We celebrated their love towards us and acknowledged our appreciation of them understanding the plan God had for our lives.

Prayer

Prayer is a huge part of preparation. We can become more prepared for our dedication journey through a lifestyle of prayer. When we pray, we reveal things about ourselves. Whatever we ask God for reveals the lack in us. Whatever we ask God for reveals He is the only source who can deliver what we need. This creates a dependency on God for everything we need and breeds trust. Even when we don't know what to do concerning our children, God does. As we draw closer to The Lord in relationship, the more we look to Him for all things. Prayer is the doorway to intimacy with The Lord. The more we commune with Him, the closer we become: we hear Him clearer, we know His ways, we respond to His Will, we obey His decrees, and we become one with Him in our actions, deeds, words, etc. Developing a lifestyle of prayer means we value connecting with God. We understand the value Jesus Christ plays in our lives, and we desire a greater relationship with Him. Plan to spend time with God and don't let anything keep you from it.

Study

We can become prepared for the dedication journey by reading and studying the Bible. As we read and study the Bible, we can ask Holy Spirit to reveal truths to us. Take notes and be serious about your spiritual growth and connection with The Lord through His Word. This will be your lifeline to true success in all areas of your life, because we can learn what God says concerning matters of life.

The Lord knows who we are raising and how we should raise them. God wants to use our children and the Bible can reveal how He can use them. Parents and guardians must have a clear understanding of God's desire to engage with children. God used children throughout the Bible (1 Samuel 3; Matthew 19:14; Ephesians 6:1; Proverbs 22:6, etc.). They are usable vessels just like adults. God certainly has a plan for them now and in the future (Jeremiah 29:11). Families should introduce a foundation of faith in Jesus that will give children a rocket boost into their calling and their purpose. Your home can be a place where the fire of God can start in the life of your child by studying the Word.

Fellowship
The growth of a spiritual family should include connections with other spiritually minded Believers. Your fellowship with others who have a similar calling and anointing is healthy for spiritual growth. Others can help prepare us for the dedication journey through their experiences and collaboration. Who you surround yourself with will make it easy or more challenging to raise your children in a godly environment. These thoughts still hold weight: *'iron sharpens iron'* and *'fools beget fools.'* The more you hang around like-minded spiritual people, the higher you will soar. People of faith encourage people of faith. People of hope encourage people of hope. I think you get the picture. So, surround yourself with powerful, positive, spirit-filled people who will help ignite the greatness in you. You choose who will be in your circle and, for the most part, who will have an influence in the

lives of your children. My husband and I had a conversation about how children think about certain things, whether it was in life, spirituality, business, community, health, finance, etc. We concluded it weighed on who their parents hung around and what they heard in conversations growing up. An example was a mastermind group who talked about speaking. The child's perspective about speaking was 'it's normal and it's what people do.' They had no fear of speaking and they had the character and traits of a good speaker at an early age. It was because they were brought up in a speaker's atmosphere. The same concept can apply in other areas (good or bad). What your children will see concerning their faith is mostly up to you. You set the stage and the table. What you allow them to be exposed to will shape and mold them. What and who you connect them with will have a large impact on their lives.

Concept 3

Who will help you during the dedication journey?

Psalm 46:1
God is our refuge and strength, an ever-present help in trouble.

First, we know The Lord is our present help. Everything we need comes from Him. He loves us so much that He sent His Son, Jesus, to redeem us from our sins (John 3:16) and to show us the way. This love is demonstrated through the acts of Jesus and the cross. After the ascension of Jesus, this same love for us is demonstrated by sending Holy Spirit to dwell with us giving us the power to overcome evil and live abundant lives. Jesus sent us the ultimate helper in His Holy Spirit. This help will equip us to do what Jesus expects us to do as His followers (John 14:26). Since we know we have a helper who will teach us all things and bring to our remembrance what the Lord has said, we can be confident The Lord will perform what He has spoken concerning us.

The Lord has also assigned other people to help us along the journey of producing Kingdom-minded children. There are other Believers who are faithful workers in the Kingdom assigned to walk with us. They can arise from our families, our churches, and our communities near and far. During baby dedications, sometimes people are named as godparents. It is unfortunate that this appointment can come just because individuals are close friends or just because families need someone to stand in to hold the *title* during the actual baby dedication ceremony. Some people receive the title of 'godparents' without knowing anything about the intent or the concept of helping in the spiritual guidance of children. Sometimes they may not even have a spiritual belief foundation of their own.

Godparents originally were people who sponsored a child's baptism and were informally responsible for ensuring a child's lifelong religious education was carried out. There are all sorts of questions about godparents: do they have legal obligations to my child, how many godparents can a child have, can you change godparents, will the godparents raise the children if the parents die, does a child even need a godparent, and do godparents have to be baptized Believers. Without getting into answering all these questions, consider a more important ideal, who to select and who not to select. If we want others to help us in the spiritual maturity of our children, it seems to be in order that they would also be *born again Believers and followers of Jesus Christ.* Amos 3:3 says, *'Can two walk together except they be agreed?* If we want others to partner with us in the spiritual guidance of our children, we must believe in the same God, the same faith, and the same baptism. The spiritual direction of our children is a serious matter. Make sure the people selected in the dedication journey have an understanding of the ending outcome of your child's salvation. We can all learn from people with skills in different areas such as business, education, trades, etc., but when it comes to selecting people to help in the spiritual maturity of our children, we want to choose those with the spiritual abilities to do so.

Too often families give unstable or non-theological ideals access to the family environment. These unstable or non-theological ideals can uproot, cause confusion, or block opportunities for God's truths to be established in the hearts of children. Don't allow chaos to infiltrate your home through the drama of ungodly vessels or media. Sexual perversion can even take place if we are not careful to shield our children through the gift of discernment provided by Holy Spirit. If children are exposed to ungodly ideals and actions, it can take root in them early, even as a baby. Infiltration can take place at any age. The enemy knows the *'early exposure concept'* too, and he will use it against us as often as he can. What our children hear, see, smell, touch, and taste are entry points to their souls. Be intentional to flood these entry points with the things of God at the earliest age possible and as often as possible.

Proverbs 18:21
The tongue has the power of life and death, and those who love it will eat its fruit.

Watch over the words you and others speak over your children. If we don't guard children from the sounds of bitter words and destructive thoughts, attempts to kill and destroy their hopes, dreams, and vision can occur.

Words are seeds of life and death. The more life seeds we plant, the more children will see the power of life through Christ. The more death seeds we plant, the further children will be pushed away from the truths of Christ. Planting more life seeds will cause the weeds of death seeds to be choked out. Make it intentional to let life seeds outgrow death seeds.

Whether it's a godparent, relative, friend, co-worker, church leader, etc., here are a few things to consider when seeking the support of others concerning your *child's spiritual growth*.

- Confirm they are a born again Believer in Jesus Christ.

- Share your beliefs and come into agreement concerning your faith expectations.

- Have a conversation discussing what you desire when it comes to your child's spiritual growth.

- Watch for a lifestyle reflecting godly character.

- Make sure they have a sincere interest in helping you.

- Make sure they express love and genuine concern for your child's spiritual advancement.

- It's helpful if they flow in their spiritual gift and they have their own discipleship plan.

- Connect with people who have raised children in the faith.

- Receive godly guidance from leaders in the church, especially pastoral and children and youth ministers.

- Seek out business and community leaders or influencer who model godliness in their respective areas.

These are all suggestions, but allow Holy Spirit to guide you with wisdom and discernment.

Ask God to help you select those who are assigned to help you in the journey of dedication. Be observant, be patient, and be obedient when it comes to selecting those who will help you during the dedication journey.

New Outlook

Write one or two things you have learned about who can help you on your dedication journey. Consider writing the actual names of those who can help you and why you have selected them. If you can't think of anyone, pray and ask The Lord to provide who He wants to help you. Be careful to listen and be patient for the right people. This may change over the years, so keep the list fresh and current.

_____

_____

_____

_____

_____

_____

Baby Dedication — It's Not About The Baby

Conclusion

A careful look at the big picture.

Baby Dedication is not about the baby, but it's about parents and guardians and the commitment they have to love, obey and honor God. Love is the key to Christian living and it is the powering force behind all that has been written in this book. Our love for God and our love for one another will keep us on the path.

How you demonstrate your understanding of the dedication process, how you prepare for the dedication journey, and how you allow others to help in the dedication journey, are decisions you will make with the help of God. Remember you are able to do this with the help of God. Your determination and excitement about your child's spiritual future is up to you.

Your child and the generations inside them will benefit from your efforts. This means generations you may never see will reap the benefits of what you invest in your child. You see, the greatest legacy we can extend to our children is the knowledge and salvation of Jesus Christ. The Gospel of Jesus Christ is the power unto salvation, the hope of glory, and the lifeline of blessings now and forever. Your obedience to train your child with the benefit of knowing The Lord will have an incredible impact on generations to come. Your commitment to this dedication journey is one of the reasons why the family exists...to reproduce godly people. Stewardship over our children means our children don't belong to us; they belong to God. We are their caretakers for just a season. Even if you have a child with special needs who may be with you all their life, our care is still for a season. What we present back to God in our children is a reflection of our devotion towards the assignment and our love towards Him.

In all the things we encounter in life, God did not guarantee us a perfect journey, but He did promise us a perfect through Christ Jesus. There will be troubles, but they won't last always. There may be a time of crisis, but The Lord will provide support through it. There may be adolescent years of bumps and bruises, but The Lord will comfort and encourage you. You won't have all the answers, but you know the God who does. You will never be alone, because The Lord promised to never leave us nor forsake us. Be encouraged because God is a promise keeper and He won't fail.

Proverbs 28:18
Where there is no vision the people will perish.

Have a vision for your family. Vision gives direction, hope and purpose. Create a family *affirmation* or *slogan* acknowledging God as the head of your family. Make sure you know you have a purpose and your children know they have a purpose. Encourage one another daily and speak blessings over your children, so one day your children will in return do the same for you.

Psalm 37:4
Delight yourself in the Lord and He will give you the desires of your heart.

When we surrender our lives unto the Will of The Lord, He will give us the desires of our hearts and this includes the desires we have for our children. Trust God with your child and know He will complete the work in them.

Enjoy the journey of dedication and know it will benefit both you and your child.

Commit your family to The Lord and seek Him with all your heart and expect to see His power work in your family.

Family Affirmation

We are a family who honors God.
We are a family who prays together.
We are a family who loves one another.
We are a family who stands together.
We are a family who serves God.

Family Slogan

We are a family and a team!

Joshua 24:15
But if serving the Lord seems undesirable to you, then choose for yourselves this day whom you will serve, whether the gods your ancestors served beyond the Euphrates, or the gods of the Amorites, in whose land you are living, but as for me and my household, we will serve the Lord.

[Special note: Post scriptures and affirmation in your home to be read on a regular basis.]

Family Goals

Our family goals will be God generated.

Our family goals will produce success glorifying God.

Our family goals will be clear and shared with everyone in the family on a regular basis.

Our family goals will reflect a home filled with love.

Our family goals will keep God and love as top priorities in our home.

Our family goals will benefit everyone in the family. (*not self-centered*)

Our family goals will reflect our godly potential.

Dedication Strategy Tips

I can start, even before birth, introducing God, Jesus, and Holy Spirit to my child.

Holy Spirit will guide me and instruct me.

The Bible is my resource book to knowing God's plan for my family.

I am equipped to do this as a Believer.

I am not alone; The Lord will never leave me no matter what it looks like.

The Lord has already given me favor and provided help.

I can speak into my child's future by confirming God's Word about my child.

I believe what God says about my child, not what the world says.

I will pray for my child daily and ask others to pray for my family.

I will not give up on my child.

I will seek God for wisdom and understanding.

I will obey God's instruction.

I will be a godly role model for my child.

I am willing to make the sacrifices necessary to ensure my child has the benefit of home and school, moral living, and knowing The Lord.

I am committed to show love and provide encouragement towards my child.

I am committed to having a no-drama zone in my home, because I will exercise the peace on God.

I will give my child the benefit of both biblical and academic education and support.

I will speak a blessing over my child regularly.

I will have daily dialogs about God in my home.

I will have family meetings and allow The Lord to govern them.

I will make Jesus the center of my family.

Plan of Action for Dedication

Who do I know as a spiritual person to encourage me as I raise my child?

What families can I model in the Bible and around me who honor God?

What will I do in my home to make sure my child knows about God, Jesus and Holy Spirit?

What steps will I take to grow as a Believer?

What is my own discipleship plan of action?

How can I strengthen my circle of spiritual influence?

When will I spend time to hear from God?

How can I grow my child who will help me grow?

How can I maintain my involvement in the life of my child?

What strategies will I put in place to raise my child as a functional adult?

New Outlook

Write one or two personal strategies you will use to better prepare yourself to carry out this assignment. Take inventory of what you know, what you don't know, and what you will do to grow. Remember, you are not alone.

_____

_____

_____

_____

_____

_____

_____

Baby Dedication — It's Not About The Baby

Scriptures to Quote Over Your Child

Cover your children with the Word of God. Memorize these scriptures or copy and place them in areas throughout your home. Speak your child's name in the blank. *(These are samples but not limited to.) (Bible sourcing.)*

Jesus is Lord in the life of _____.
(Phil. 2:10-11)

_____ is more than a conqueror.
(Romans 8:37)

_____ can do all things through Christ which strengthens her/him.
(Phil. 4:13)

_____ is the head and not the tail.
(Deut. 28:13)

_____ increases in wisdom and favor with God and man.
(Luke 2:52)

_____ is an overcomer because he/she is born of God.
(1 John 5:4)

_____ obeys his/her parents and he/she will live a long life.
(Eph. 6:1-3)

_____ is led by his/her inner man: He/she obeys God's voice.
(John 10:27)

_____ is redeemed from the curse of the law. Jesus bore his/her sickness and carried his/her disease. _____'s body operates in perfection as it was created to.
(Gal. 3:13 & Matt. 8:17)

_____ is a disciple of Jesus Christ; taught of The Lord and obedient to His will. Great is his/her peace and undisturbed composure.
(Isaiah 54:13)

Prayers for Your Child

There are many scriptures referring to the importance of prayer. It is important to teach children how to pray. As part of their learning, let prayers and scriptures found in the Word guide them. Teach them how to pray from their hearts and learn to talk to God to build their relationship with Him.

Include the following to start (also research the five-finger prayer concepts):

1. Give thanks (express the love you have for God)
2. Ask for forgiveness (repent of known and unknown sins)
3. Petition (ask for help, favor, protection, wisdom, etc. for yourself)
4. Pray for the lost (salvation of souls)
5. Pray for others (intercession)

Matthew 6:9-13

After this manner therefore pray ye:
Our Father which art in heaven, Hallowed be thy name. Thy kingdom come, Thy will be done in earth, as it is in heaven. Give us this day our daily bread. And forgive us our debts, as we forgive our debtors. And lead us not into temptation, but deliver us from evil: For thine is the kingdom, and the power, and the glory, forever. Amen.

Psalm 23

The Lord is my shepherd, I lack nothing. He makes me lie down in green pastures, He leads me beside quiet waters, He refreshes my soul. He guides me along the right paths for His name's sake. Even though I walk through the darkest valley, I will fear no evil, for You are with me; Your rod and Your staff, they comfort me. You prepare a table before me in the presence of my enemies. You anoint my head with oil; my cup overflows. Surely Your goodness and love will follow me all the days of my life, and I will dwell in the house of the Lord forever.

John 17

Share this chapter in John as a foundation to understand how Jesus prayed.

Prayers to Pray over Your Child

Pray these prayers over your children to cover, strengthen and protect them. Pray for their needs and desires often. Pray prayers to build them up in the Lord (wisdom, courage, obedience, blessings, salvation, protection, mental and physical health, prosperity, forgiveness, responsibility, accountability, confidence, strength, joy, peace, fulfillment, etc.). [Put your child's name in the blank spaces to make it personal.]

Prayer of Blessing

Numbers 6:24-26
"The Lord bless _____ and keep _____; the Lord make His face shine on _____ and be gracious to _____; the Lord turn His face toward _____ and give _____ peace." In Jesus' name, Amen.

Prayer of Protection

In the name of Jesus, we/I declare and decree spiritual safety over, _____. We/I speak divine protection from every satanic force sent against _____. We/I silence every curse sent against our family and rebuke the tongue of the devourer. We/I renounce all interaction and communication with evil spirits. No weapon formed against _____ shall prosper. We/I pronounce protection by the blood of Jesus over _____. Thank You Lord for hearing this prayer and for protecting Your child, _____. In Jesus' name, Amen.

Prayer of Success

Psalm 27: 1
The Lord is _____'s light and salvation, _____ shall not fear anyone. The Lord is the strength of _____'s life and he/she shall not be afraid. The Lord will watch over and keep _____ in his/her going out and

coming in. The Lord will bless _____ with ideas and inventions to create wealth. The Lord will watch over the success of _____ and keep him/her in perfect peace.

Jeremiah 29:11

_____ knows the Lord has plans for him/her; plans to prosper and not to harm, plans to give hope and a future. _____ trusts the Lord in these plans. We/I speak blessings and protection over _____'s future and nothing can stop the plans the Lord has for _____. We/I declare and decree success in faith, health, wealth, wisdom, relationships, and opportunities. We/I speak favor and blessings towards _____ all the days of his/her life. We/I consider this established and done in the name of Jesus, Amen.

The Prayer of the Blessing of Abraham

Genesis 12:2-3

The Lord will lead _____ to his/her promised place. The Lord will make his/her name great and he/she will be a blessing. The Lord will bless those who bless _____, and whoever curses him/her He will curse. The Lord will allow people to be blessed through _____. In Jesus' name, Amen.

Leading Your Child to Jesus Christ (Salvation)

ABCs of Salvation (<u>A</u>dmit we are sinners, <u>B</u>elieve in Jesus Christ, and <u>C</u>onfess our sins and repent)

One of the greatest privileges we have is leading our own children to Jesus Christ. Ask God to prepare your child's heart to receive the Good News of Jesus and to prepare you to communicate His Word effectively to them. Don't worry about their age, but let Holy Spirit guide you and your child. *(Let the children come to Jesus and do not hinder them. Matthew 19:14)*

Something as important as a child's personal relationship with Jesus Christ requires special attention. Talk to your child about salvation and know that children should respond individually to salvation. This response should be genuine. Make sure children understand this is a personal response and it should not be to please peers, parents, teachers, etc.; it is an act of the heart.

Make sure your child is clear about salvation when the time comes. Sometime we ask people if they are "saved" which may be vague. Some may wonder, saved from what? Try asking and teaching, "Have you asked Jesus to be your Savior and Lord?" (Lord/Surrendering our will to His will; Savior/saving us from the penalty of our sins.) Then offer the specifics about salvation.

Suggested concepts for a child's salvation:

1. God wants you to become a part of His eternal family. (John 1:12; 1 John 4:8)

2. We all have sinned against God, but He still loves us. (Romans 3:23)

3. God loves us so much that He sent His Son, Jesus, to die on the cross for our sins. Because Jesus never sinned, He was the only one who could take our punishment for sin (John 3:16; 15:3; John 4:14); Jesus died for our sins, but God raised Jesus from the dead and He is alive forever. (Romans 10:9)

4. We can receive Jesus as our Savior, tell God we are sorry for our sins, and ask for His forgiveness. (1 John 1:9)

5. When we believe in Jesus, we receive God's gift of eternal life. (1 John 2:24-25)

6. As Believers, we become the children of God. (Galatians 3:26)

Rejoice when your child receives Jesus Christ as Savior and Lord because their names are written in the Lamb's Book of Life. (Luke 10:20)

When leading children to Jesus Christ, we want them to know the scriptures concerning their salvation. *(You can also incorporate the "Roman's Road" scriptures.)*

WAY to salvation... John 14:6 "Jesus said unto him, I am the way, the truth and the life; no man comes unto the Father, but by Me"

*WHY we are saved...*John 3:16 "For God so loved the world that He gave His only begotten Son, that whoever believes in Him should not perish but have everlasting life"

*HOW we become saved...*Romans 10:9 "if you confess with your mouth the Lord Jesus and believe in your heart that God has raised Him from the dead, you will be saved"

WHAT we do when we are saved...Mark 16:16 "He who believes and is baptized will be saved; but he who does not believe will be condemned"

A sample Repentance and Salvation Prayer:

Lord Jesus, I believe You love me, come into my life and make me a new creature. I confess I am a sinner and need a Savior. I surrender my life to You. I ask You to forgive me of my sins and help me to walk with You. I believe You are the Son of God sent to save the world. I believe You died for my sins and God raised You from the dead. Thank You for loving me, for saving me, and for Your abundant grace. Thank You for giving me eternal life. Amen

What We Believe

Define what you believe and make sure you communicate it often with your children. The old saying, 'if you don't stand for something, you will fall for anything,' can be true in this instance. The enemy continues to heap on us lies not representing what God says. Building strong foundations require us to create conversations to share what we believe.

We believe in One God, One Faith, and One Baptism (Ephesians 4:4-6)

We believe Jesus is the son of God. (John 3:16)

We believe Jesus died for the sins of the world. (1 John 2:2)

We believe Jesus is alive and sits at the right hand of the Father. (Mark 16:19)

The Bible - We believe the entire Bible is inspired by God, without error and the authority on which we base our faith and life. The Bible is a written record of God revealing Himself through creation, history and Jesus Christ. The Bible is God speaking to us.

The Trinity - We believe in one God who exists in three distinct persons: Father, Son and Holy Spirit.

Salvation - We believe Jesus died on the cross and shed His blood for our sins. We believe salvation is found by placing our faith in what Jesus did for us on the cross. We believe Jesus rose from the dead and is coming again.

Water Baptism - We believe water baptism is a symbol of the cleansing power of the blood of Jesus Christ and a testimony to our faith in the Lord Jesus Christ.

Communion (The Lord's Supper) - We believe in the regular taking of Communion as an act of remembering what the Lord Jesus did for us on the cross.

Growing Relationship - We believe every believer should be in a growing relationship with Jesus by obeying God's Word, yielding to Holy Spirit, and being conformed to the image of Jesus Christ.

A Spiritual Outlook Plan

A roadmap for your child's spiritual journey will allow your child to experience the love of God through Jesus Christ, to have a personal encounter with Holy Spirit, and grow as a disciple. The spiritual outlook is a progressive plan, building from one level to the next to help grow you and your child as you move from one phase of life to another. Always be willing to review the needs of your child as they grow. They change and so do you. Each child is different and learns differently. Make sure you observe and know the learning styles of your child.

Have a general plan of action on what you want your child to receive spiritually as they grow older. Don't force fit, but be intentional to talk about what you want your children to know. Consider this: you don't know what they know until you have taught them or seen the fruit they bear concerning the things you want them to know. Having engaging conversations that create dialog is a healthy environment for learning. The environment we want to create is an environment where the child wants to return for more.

Basic Examples…

Age 0-3 Demonstrate the concepts of prayer and worship. Begin their biblical language as you build their earthly language (know how to say Jesus, God, Holy Spirit, etc.; demonstrate expressions of love, kindness, helping, etc.)

Age 4-6 Expand prayer and worship to develop a foundational relationship with God. Know Bible stories and how the love of God is demonstrated in the stories. Put your family in the posture to relate to some of the stories and discuss how God works in your family and in the lives of other people. Explore your child's spiritual gifts and expose their abilities.

Age 7-9 Continue prayer and worship. Build on the concepts of the Bible, nurture spiritual gifts, and include worship and praise to the Lord. Grow spiritual life principles to help develop their faith and belief system in the Lord.

Age 10-12 Strengthen prayer. Work of spiritual life skills and biblical modeling for others. Teach them how to witness through their living and experiences.

Age 13-16 Continue to build on prayer. Develop a serving character in the Kingdom and develop discipleship principles.

Age 17-21 Let them test their wings in what they have learned as they launch out. Become a guide, advisor and coach to help them stay on course.

Age 22+ Let them soar and continue to cover them in prayer and be a watchman to offer support, encouragement, advice, and spiritual guidance.

All of these layers should continue as building blocks throughout your child's life and into their adulthood. This will help them develop a solid relationship with The Lord.

This is only a guide to help you get an idea about creating a *spiritual outlook* for your child. You will have to add much more as The Lord reveals it to you regarding your own child. Pay attention to your child; ask them questions about their thoughts, their dreams, their goals, and their emotions. Know when you need to love more and when to guide more. Every child is different, but God knows who they are and who they will become, so seek His guidance daily. Ask The Lord, 'WHO AM I RAISING?,' then *wait* and *watch* to hear and see. He has all the answers.

Prayer for Families

Father, I thank you for the gift of family. I praise You for planning family from the beginning and how You have addressed every concern. I thank You for allowing children to be born in the earth. Now Lord, help us to be good stewards over those You have placed in our care. Open our eyes, so we may see the value in children and the value in us as we parent and guide them. Give us creative ways to share Your Word with our children and let Your Word occupy a burning passion in our hearts as we share it with our children. Give us a hunger to succeed in discipling our own children and other children and youth in our reach. Let us have a clear understanding about the role we play when it comes to the commitment of dedicating our children to You. Let us complete our assignment with our children, so we may hear, 'Well done good and faithful servant.' Allow our efforts to raise our children in a spiritual environment be pleasing to You, Father. Holy Spirit we ask for your help, so we will not become weary in this work. Help us cast every care upon You, Lord. We trust You will provide and care for us in every area of our lives. Lord, we thank You for the gift of children and the joy they bring to us. We thank You for blessing us and adding no sorrow.

Thank You for blessing every parent and guardian who reads this prayer and this book. Give them strength to endure until the end. Thank You, Father, for their lives. Keep them, so they will be kept. Lord we love You and we honor You with our living and the fruit of our lips. Thank You for hearing our prayers and responding in the way You know is best for us. Thank You, Lord, for Your divine protection. Grant us and our children good health, longevity, and a more abundant life. In the name of Jesus, Amen.

AUTHOR

Rosemary Winbush has served as a Pastor and leader in the ministry for children and has more than 30 years of experience in this ministry area. She writes published curriculum for the children and preteen ministry and leads a team of more than 250 volunteers. She has developed a strong spiritually based children and preteen ministry and created a core structure with specialized leadership teams. Rosemary's ministry extends beyond the walls of her place of worship as she strives to promote and enhance the spiritual and social growth of children across the globe. She has developed targeted programs which are hosted in elementary schools and other organizations focusing on children. Rosemary is the co-founder of a *Children's Ministry International* prayer movement and she is also the founder of *The7Movement*, a biblical study group for women. She is the author of *Essentials to Start, Build, and Refresh Children's Ministry* and the producer of *Live Healing for Children*.

Rosemary is a licensed, ordained minister. She has presented to children and preteens, children's ministry leaders and workers, families and other groups at special training sessions, conferences, and worship services. Rosemary continuously expands her biblical knowledge, because she desires to more effectively share the Gospel of Jesus Christ with children.

Rosemary and her husband, Wyman, have three adult children.

Connect for ministry and other resources

Kairos International
Jacksonville, Florida
www.rosemarywinbush.com

Wyman and Rosemary Winbush are owners of Kairos International. They are committed to educating, empowering and inspiring individuals to reach their maximum and divine potential.

With over 40 years of combined leadership experience and skills, Wyman and Rosemary are able to leverage their expertise to provide spiritual teaching to meet the needs of individuals through special ministry presentations, personal and group coaching, special resources and prayer.

Made in the USA
Lexington, KY
12 November 2019